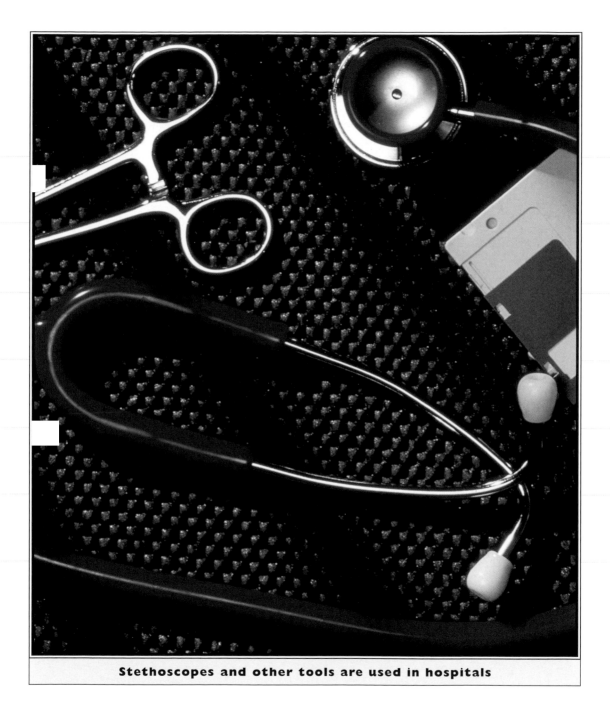

**Stethoscopes and other tools are used in hospitals**

# A Hospital

**Natalie Rosinsky**

A⁺

**Smart Apple Media**

∽ Published by Smart Apple Media

1980 Lookout Drive, North Mankato, MN 56003

Designed by Rita Marshall

Copyright © 2004 Smart Apple Media. International copyright reserved in all countries. No part of this book may be reproduced in any form without written permission from the publisher.

Printed in the United States of America

∽ Photographs by Corbis (David Pollack), Tom Myers, Tom Stack & Associates (Novastock, Tom & Therisa Stack, TSADO/NASA), Unicorn Stock Photos (Jeff Greenberg)

∽ Library of Congress Cataloging-in-Publication Data

Rosinsky, Natalie M. (Natalie Myra). A hospital / by Natalie Rosinsky.

p. cm. — (Field trips) Includes bibliographical references and index.

Summary: Introduces what different parts of a hospital are like, who the people are that work in hospitals, what special equipment is used to care for patients, and what all hospitals have in common.

∽ ISBN 1-58340-327-2

1. Hospitals—Juvenile literature. [1. Hospitals.] I. Title. II. Field trips (Smart Apple Media) (Mankato, Minn.).

RA963.5.R675 2003     362.1'1—dc21     2002042781

∽ First Edition  9 8 7 6 5 4 3 2 1

# A Hospital

CONTENTS

## A Small City

Visitors to a hospital may be grateful for its city-like signs and maps. Even the smallest hospital is divided into many different spaces. A large hospital may spread across several buildings. It may be easy to get lost! Because **ambulances** must reach it quickly, the emergency room is near a front or side entrance. Accident victims and other people with emergencies receive help there. The maternity section, where women have babies, is also near an entrance.

Hospitals may be large buildings many stories high

Babies sometimes arrive in a hurry! Speed is not important for food or laundry deliveries. These spaces are located at the back, or in the basement. Hospitals have many rooms with beds for patients. There are also operating rooms, in which **surgery** is performed. Medicines are kept in the pharmacy. The physical therapy area is where patients can exercise. Patients younger than 16 stay in a separate area. It even has a playroom and schoolroom!

**The word "hospital" is related to the word "hotel." Both come from a Latin word meaning "to welcome guests."**

**Operating rooms have a lot of high-tech equipment**

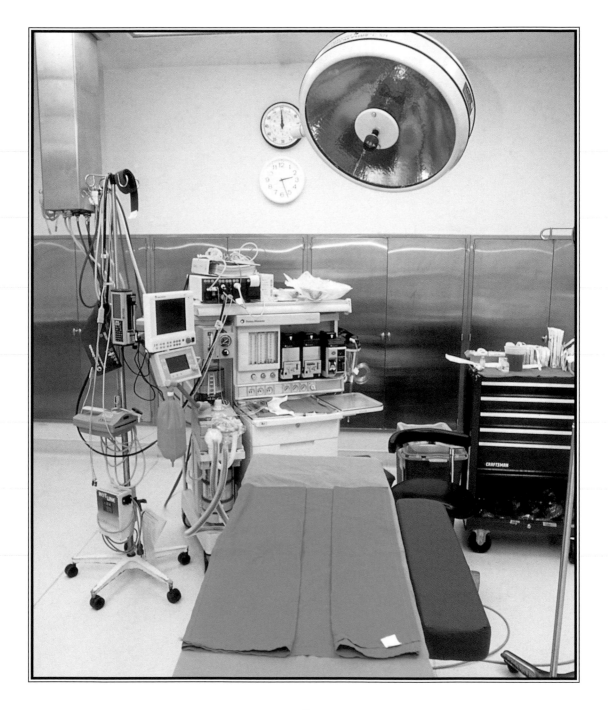

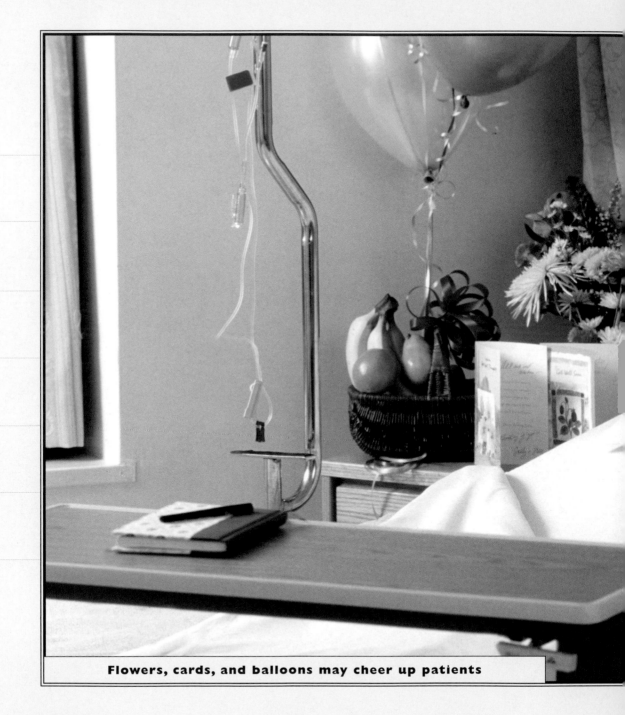

**Flowers, cards, and balloons may cheer up patients**

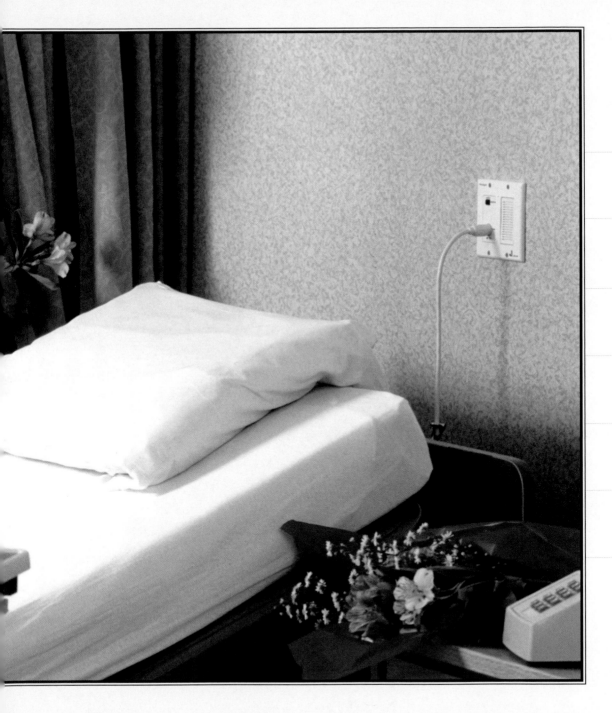

## Helping Hands

A hospital never sleeps. People work there around the clock, including many doctors. There are special kinds of doctors, such as doctors who work only on people's hearts or doctors who help only children. Others, called interns and residents, are still learning to be doctors. ⌘ Nurses give patients medicine, make them comfortable, and check up on them. A nurse is often the first person to help a patient in trouble. Physical therapists work with patients who are getting better. Patients may need to exercise to get stronger after

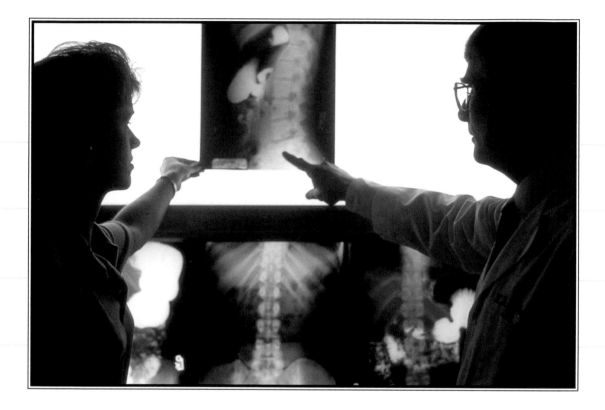

accidents or surgery. Medical technicians examine small

samples of blood and other body products. Their work helps

doctors to **diagnose** a patient's problems. ᏧᎳ Clerks make

**Doctors look at x-rays to learn how to help patients**

sure that medical records, which contain information about patients and their illnesses, are all correct and up-to-date.

Dieticians plan healthy meals for patients. Patients may never meet a hospital's many food, laundry, and maintenance workers. Yet without their helping hands, a hospital could not exist. Keeping a hospital clean is very important to prevent **diseases** from spreading.

## Tools and Machines

There are many types of special equipment in a hospital to diagnose a patient's problems. These tools may be simple,

such as the metal and rubber stethoscope used to hear heart

and lung sounds. Other tools are complicated, such as the

machines used to see inside a patient's body. Hospitals use

**Medical technicians test patient samples for diseases**

equipment to examine patients' blood and other samples. Sometimes, only a few test tubes are needed. Other tests may require special electronic machines and computers. If a patient needs surgery, he or she is wheeled into and out of the operating room on a **gurney**. In surgery, sharp knives called scalpels are used to cut

**Hospitals once had a bad reputation. Before people learned more about diseases, most hospital patients died.**

into the patient. Machines are used to supply the patient with air or medicine. In physical therapy, a patient may use special equipment to strengthen or stretch different body parts.

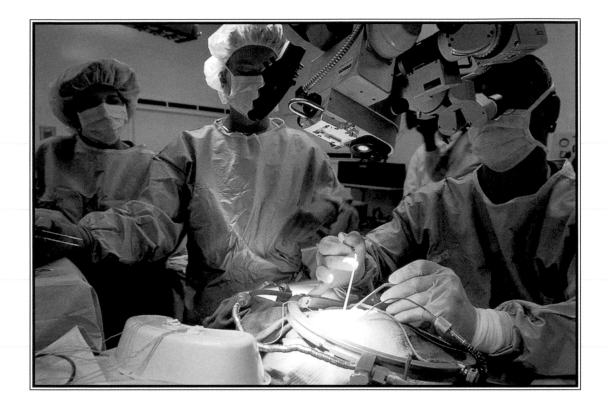

Because swimming may be part of therapy, some hospitals

even have their own swimming pools!  Hospitals also

supply equipment to make daily routines easier for patients

and nurses. Hospital beds move up and down. Bedpans help patients who cannot move enough to get to a bathroom.

Wheelchairs, walkers, and crutches help some patients move around. Instead of frequent shots, patients may get medicine through tubes kept in their arms.

## From Sickness to Health

A few hospitals treat only one kind of disease. Some hospitals treat only sick children. Most hospitals help people of all ages with any kind of medical problem. All hospitals are exciting places to visit, filled with workers and equipment

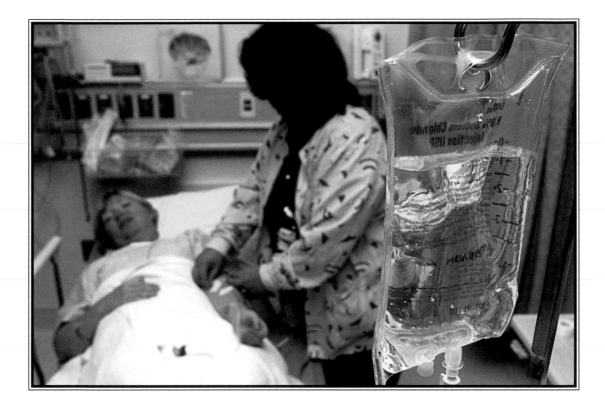

devoted to helping sick people get well. A hospital can

be a very busy place. The waiting rooms are crowded with

people who need to see a doctor. Hallways are filled with

Medicine runs through a tube into this patient's arm

patients being wheeled into surgery or taken to physical ther-

apy. Food, laundry, cleaning supplies, and medical equipment

are also wheeled around the hallways. If people are not care-

ful, they may bump into one another! **Until the 1800s, most doctors did not go to medical school. They learned their skills by working with other exper-ienced doctors.**

Doctors, nurses, and technicians move quickly to get to an emergency. Patients' friends and family carrying

flowers and balloons add to the unending traffic in the small

city that is a hospital.

**Hospitals are large, busy places full of caring people**

# A Sign of Health

Doctors and nurses count the number of times the heart beats each minute to pump blood. This is called the heart rate. If a patient's heart is beating too fast or too slow, he or she may be in danger.

## What You Need

A clock with a second hand

## What You Do

1. Put the tip of your index finger on your wrist, just below the thumb.
2. Move your finger slightly until you feel the soft beat.
3. Look at the clock. Count the number of beats you feel in 30 seconds.
4. Multiply this number by two. The result is your heart rate.

## What You See

For children, a healthy heart beats between 70 and 110 times every minute. Adults have slower hearts. Sitting still, a healthy adult has a heart rate of 60 to 80 beats per minute.

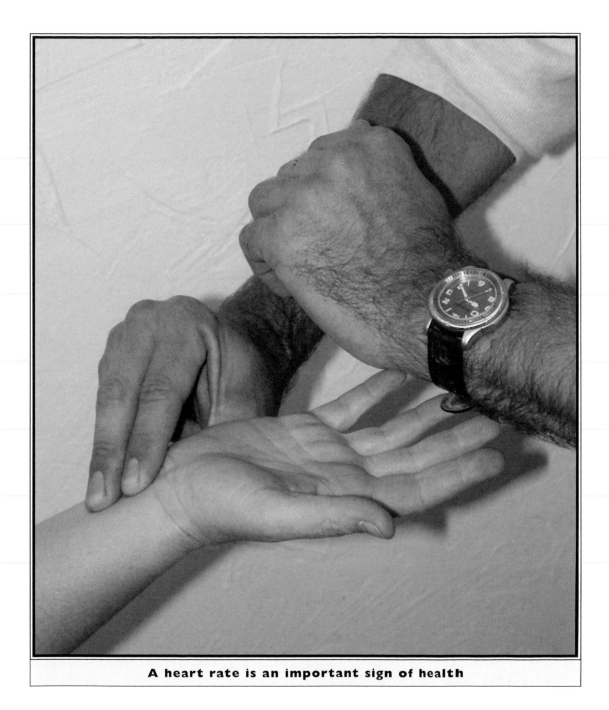

**A heart rate is an important sign of health**

## Index

## Words to Know

**ambulances** (AM-byoo-lens-ez)—small trucks with medical equipment that rush accident victims and sick people to hospitals

**diagnose** (dy-ag-NOHS)—to figure out the cause of an illness or medical problem

**diseases** (di-ZEEZ-ez)—different kinds of sickness, sometimes spread from one person to another

**emergency** (ee-MUR-jen-see)—a dangerous problem that must be fixed right away

**gurney** (GUR-nee)—a bed with wheels; used to move a patient around the hospital

**surgery** (SUR-jur-ee)—cutting into a patient's body to make him or her better

## Read More

Howe, James. *The Hospital Book*. New York: William Morrow, 1994.

Malam, John. *Hospital: From Accident and Emergency to X-Ray*. New York: Peter Bedrick Books, 1999.

Masoff, Joy. *Emergency!* New York: Scholastic Books, 1999.

## Internet Sites

Going on a Hospital Tour
http://www.faculty.fairfield.edu/
fleitas/hospital.html

Going to the Hospital
http://www.kidshealth.org/kid/
feel_better/places/hospital.html

Helping Children Cope with the
Intensive Care Unit
http://www.vh.org/Patients/IHB/Peds/
Psych/ICU/Hello3Kids.html

The Hospital for Sick Children
http://www.sickkids.on.ca